Alberta D. Jones

# *MONACO 2*

## *GAME GUIDE*

*Unlock Hidden Levels, Outsmart Security,
and Execute Flawless Heists*

# Chapter 1: Introduction to Monaco 2

## 1.1 What is Monaco 2?

*Monaco 2* is the long-awaited sequel to the critically acclaimed heist game, *Monaco: What's Yours Is Mine*. Developed by *Pocketwatch Games*, this action-packed cooperative title builds on its predecessor while introducing new features, mechanics, and a fresh visual style.

### Overview

In *Monaco 2*, players once again take on the role of various unique characters as they plan and execute daring heists. Set in a vibrant, immersive world, the game combines stealth, strategy, and puzzle-solving elements, making each heist feel like a carefully orchestrated mission. With the addition of new gameplay mechanics, updated graphics, and more intricate level designs, *Monaco 2* promises to be a thrilling experience for both new players and veterans of the original game.

### Storyline

The narrative in *Monaco 2* picks up after the events of the first game, taking players through a series of missions that span a variety of environments. While specific plot details remain scarce, it is clear that players will be immersed in a world filled with intrigue, danger, and the constant threat of being caught. The game explores the world of high-stakes heists, featuring a colorful cast of characters with their own backstories and motivations.

## Gameplay Innovations

While retaining the core mechanics that made the original *Monaco* so appealing, *Monaco 2* introduces several new features:

- **3D Environments**: The game transitions from the 2D top-down perspective of the original to fully rendered 3D environments, offering players a more dynamic and immersive experience.

- **Procedurally Generated Levels**: Each heist is now more unpredictable, with procedurally generated levels ensuring that no two missions are the same.

- **Expanded Character Roster**: A wider variety of playable characters with unique abilities and skill sets allows for greater flexibility in planning and executing heists.

- **New Tools & Gadgets**: Players can utilize a range of new tools and gadgets, from advanced hacking devices to explosive traps, adding complexity and strategic depth to each mission.

## Visual Style & Aesthetic

The game's visual style is a blend of modern 3D graphics with the charming, cartoonish aesthetic that the original *Monaco* was known for. While maintaining a colorful and whimsical tone, the updated visuals enhance the game's sense of immersion and give it a more polished look. The lighting and environmental effects are more dynamic, helping create tension during sneaky infiltrations or high-octane escapes.

## Multiplayer and Co-op Experience

One of the standout features of *Monaco 2* is its emphasis on cooperative multiplayer gameplay. Players can team up online or locally to tackle heists together, each taking on a different role within the team. Whether sneaking past guards, hacking security systems, or carrying out the heist's main objective, teamwork is essential to success. Communication and coordination are key, and the game offers tools to facilitate this during gameplay.

## Why It's Exciting

For fans of the original *Monaco*, the sequel promises to deliver an even more engaging experience, while newcomers will find an accessible, fun, and challenging game that offers something for everyone. The combination of strategic planning, thrilling action, and the need for cooperation makes *Monaco 2* a unique and compelling addition to the co-op action genre.

With its innovative new features, *Monaco 2* is shaping up to be one of the most anticipated titles for heist game enthusiasts. Whether you're playing solo or with friends, the game invites you to engage in high-stakes, fast-paced heists where every decision counts.

# 1.2 Key Differences from Monaco: What's Yours Is Mine

While *Monaco 2* maintains the core elements that made the original *Monaco: What's Yours Is Mine* a hit—such as cooperative gameplay, stealth mechanics, and heist-themed action—there are several notable differences that distinguish the two games. These changes elevate the experience, improve gameplay dynamics, and offer new challenges for both returning players and newcomers.

## 1.3D Environments vs. 2D Top-Down View

One of the most significant changes in *Monaco 2* is the shift from the original's 2D top-down perspective to fully 3D environments.

- **Monaco (2013)**: The original game employed a 2D, top-down camera perspective, giving it a more minimalist and retro-style feel. This approach allowed for quick and easy navigation through its maps and an overhead view of the action.

- **Monaco 2**: With the sequel, players are immersed in a more visually dynamic world with fully rendered 3D environments. This change allows for better depth, improved lighting effects, and more intricate level designs. Players now have more freedom in how they interact with the environment and can use the verticality of the levels to their advantage, such as climbing structures or hiding behind objects.

The 3D shift brings a more realistic and immersive experience, offering a fresh take on familiar mechanics.

## 2. Procedurally Generated Levels

In *Monaco 2*, each heist is generated with procedural algorithms, meaning the levels are not fixed and will differ each time you play.

- **Monaco (2013)**: The original game had pre-designed, fixed levels where players could memorize layouts and learn optimal strategies over time. While this allowed for a deep understanding of each map, it limited replayability once players became familiar with the environment.

- **Monaco 2**: With procedurally generated levels, every mission in *Monaco 2* feels unique. The map layout, enemy placements, security measures, and even objectives are randomized, which ensures that players will face different challenges every time they play. This change increases replayability and keeps the game feeling fresh, even for veteran players.

## 3. Expanded Character Roster and Abilities

While the original *Monaco* featured a small selection of characters, each with unique abilities, *Monaco 2* significantly expands the roster and deepens character customization.

- **Monaco (2013)**: The original game had eight playable characters, each with one special ability—such as the Hacker, who could bypass security, or the Gentleman, who could distract guards. These abilities were simple but effective, creating a varied gameplay experience depending on the character chosen.

- **Monaco 2**: The sequel introduces a broader and more diverse cast of characters, each with more specialized and customizable abilities. In addition to traditional roles, *Monaco 2* introduces new classes that bring more versatility to heist planning. For example, players may now have the option to choose characters who can blend into their surroundings, manipulate the environment more effectively, or utilize advanced tech to disable or hack enemy systems. With more characters to choose from and more complex abilities, players will have more tactical options when planning and executing their heists.

## 4. New Tools and Gadgets

The toolkit in *Monaco 2* is more extensive and varied than the one in the original game, giving players new ways to approach each mission.

- **Monaco (2013)**: Tools in the original game were relatively simple and focused on the basic elements of heists. Tools like lockpicks, smoke bombs, and distractions were key to staying undetected and successfully completing objectives. The variety was somewhat limited but allowed for creative uses in heist planning.

- **Monaco 2**: The sequel introduces a larger array of high-tech gadgets and tools that add new layers of strategy to heist planning. New options include advanced hacking devices, explosive charges, EMPs, and more. The use of these tools requires careful planning and coordination, making each heist feel more complex and requiring players to think outside the box. Some gadgets even interact with the environment in dynamic ways, like disabling cameras or disabling security systems with a single device.

## 5. Enhanced AI and Enemy Behavior

AI behavior has been significantly improved in *Monaco 2*, providing a more challenging and responsive experience.

- **Monaco (2013)**: While the AI in the original game was competent, guards and enemies followed basic routines and were relatively easy to predict. Once players had memorized patrol patterns, it became easier to avoid detection.

- **Monaco 2**: In *Monaco 2*, the AI is more advanced, with enemies reacting more intelligently to player actions. Guards may communicate with each other when they spot a suspicious movement, or even work in teams to corner the player. The game also includes more advanced security systems that players will have to outsmart, such as automated drones, facial recognition systems, and more complex alarm mechanisms. This enhanced AI pushes players to be more cautious and strategic during their heists.

## 6. Cooperative and Multiplayer Enhancements

While both *Monaco* games feature co-op play, *Monaco 2* builds on this feature by offering a deeper and more refined multiplayer experience.

- **Monaco (2013)**: The original game allowed for both local and online multiplayer with up to four players, and the focus was on working together to pull off heists. While fun, the cooperative gameplay was sometimes challenging due to the limitations of the controls and communication tools.

- **Monaco 2**: *Monaco 2* takes multiplayer to the next level by adding refined communication tools, better matchmaking systems, and more robust multiplayer options. Players can now better coordinate their actions, whether they're sneaking through a security system or carrying out an explosive distraction. The game also introduces new multiplayer game modes that enhance replayability and challenge. These modes are designed to foster cooperation, ensuring that each member of the team has a vital role to play.

## 7. Overall Aesthetic and Presentation

Finally, the visual and aesthetic style of *Monaco 2* is more polished, providing a modern look while still retaining the charm of the original.

- **Monaco (2013)**: The original game had a pixel-art, top-down aesthetic that was simple but effective. Its retro style gave the game a unique feel, but it sometimes lacked the depth and complexity seen in other modern games.

- **Monaco 2**: The sequel has moved to a fully 3D art style with more realistic textures, improved lighting effects, and a more immersive world. While still colorful and whimsical, *Monaco 2* offers a more visually dynamic experience, where the environments feel alive and react to the player's actions in new ways. This upgrade in presentation makes the game feel more cinematic and engaging.

# 1.3 Supported Platforms & System Requirements

## Supported Platforms

*Monaco 2* will be available on a wide range of platforms, allowing players from various gaming ecosystems to dive into the action-packed world of heists. The game supports both single-player and cooperative multiplayer modes, and it will be available on:

- **PC (Windows)**

- **PlayStation 4**

- **PlayStation 5**

- **Xbox One**

- **Xbox Series X|S**

- **Nintendo Switch**

In addition, *Monaco 2* will be available through several digital distribution services, including:

- **Steam** (PC)

- **Epic Games Store** (PC)

- **PlayStation Store** (PS4/PS5)

- **Microsoft Store** (Xbox)

- **Nintendo eShop** (Switch)

This wide support ensures that *Monaco 2* will be accessible to a broad range of players across multiple gaming platforms.

## System Requirements for PC

For PC players, *Monaco 2* will have specific system requirements to ensure smooth performance. The game has been designed to run on a variety of machines, from lower-end setups to high-end gaming rigs, but performance will be best on more powerful hardware. Here's what you'll need:

**Minimum System Requirements**

These are the baseline specifications required to run *Monaco 2* on your PC:

- **OS**: Windows 10 (64-bit)

- **Processor**: Intel Core i5-7400 / AMD Ryzen 3 2200G

- **Memory**: 8 GB RAM

- **Graphics**: NVIDIA GTX 1050 / AMD Radeon RX 560

- **DirectX**: Version 11

- **Storage**: 20 GB available space

- **Network**: Broadband Internet connection (for online multiplayer)

With these minimum specifications, you can expect to play *Monaco 2* with decent performance, though you may need to lower certain graphical settings for smoother gameplay on lower-end hardware.

**Recommended System Requirements**

For the best possible experience with high graphics settings, fast loading times, and stable frame rates, these are the recommended specs:

- **OS**: Windows 10 or 11 (64-bit)

- **Processor**: Intel Core i7-8700K / AMD Ryzen 5 3600X

- **Memory**: 16 GB RAM

- **Graphics**: NVIDIA RTX 2060 / AMD Radeon RX 5700 XT

- **DirectX**: Version 12

- **Storage**: 25 GB available space (SSD recommended for faster load times)

- **Network**: Broadband Internet connection (for multiplayer)

With these recommended specifications, you'll experience smooth gameplay, high-quality graphics, and optimal performance during both single-player and multiplayer sessions.

### Graphics Settings & Optimization Tips

If you find that the game is not running as smoothly as you'd like, there are several in-game settings you can adjust to improve performance. Lowering settings such as shadow quality, anti-aliasing, and texture resolution can help maintain a steady frame rate, especially on systems that meet the minimum specifications.

## Console Requirements

For those playing on consoles, the game is optimized for both previous and current-generation systems. Here's what you need for each platform:

- **PlayStation 4 & Xbox One**: The game runs at 30 FPS and 1080p resolution, providing smooth performance for last-generation consoles.

- **PlayStation 5 & Xbox Series X|S**: On these newer consoles, *Monaco 2* will run at 60 FPS and in 4K resolution on compatible devices, providing a more visually polished and fluid experience.

On consoles, there's no need for specific configurations, as the game will automatically adjust to the system's capabilities. However, having the latest system software updates installed is recommended for optimal performance.

## Cross-Platform Play

One of the exciting features of *Monaco 2* is cross-platform multiplayer support. Players can team up with friends regardless of whether they are on PC, PlayStation, Xbox, or Switch. This feature enhances the game's cooperative multiplayer experience, ensuring that no matter which platform you're using, you can join forces with others.

## Additional Notes

- **Cloud Saves**: For PC players, *Monaco 2* will support cloud saves through Steam and Epic Games Store, meaning you can pick up where you left off, even when switching devices.

- **Online Multiplayer**: A stable internet connection is required for playing in co-op multiplayer mode, particularly for online sessions.

- **VR Support**: At launch, *Monaco 2* does not feature VR support. However, the developers have hinted at possible future updates that may include VR compatibility.

# 1.4 Game Modes & Multiplayer Options

*Monaco 2* offers a variety of game modes and multiplayer options that ensure every playthrough feels fresh and exciting. Whether you prefer to tackle heists alone or join forces with friends, there's a mode suited for all types of players. Let's take a look at the available game modes and the multiplayer features that make *Monaco 2* an exciting experience.

## 1. Single-Player Mode

For those who prefer to go solo, *Monaco 2* includes a robust single-player mode where you can embark on heists, solve puzzles, and engage with the game's story at your own pace. The single-player experience offers a deep, immersive journey as you control a team of unique characters, each with their own special abilities.

- **Story Mode**: This is the heart of *Monaco 2*'s single-player content. Players follow the narrative, executing increasingly complex heists as they advance through levels. The story is rich in lore, and each mission introduces new challenges and gameplay mechanics. Players can complete missions in various ways, including using stealth or brute force, depending on the character they choose and their approach to the heist.

- **Replayability**: While you're playing solo, you can replay levels multiple times to experiment with different characters and strategies. Since the levels are procedurally generated, no two playthroughs are the same. This keeps the single-player experience exciting and offers players a chance to master their skills and achieve higher scores.

## 2. Co-Op Multiplayer Mode

Cooperative multiplayer is the core of *Monaco 2*, where players team up to pull off heists. This mode emphasizes teamwork and communication, as each player controls a different character with unique abilities, requiring coordination to successfully complete the mission.

- **Up to 4 Players**: You can team up with up to three other players to plan and execute heists. The more players you have, the more strategies and tactics become available, making each mission feel dynamic. The synergy between different character abilities, such as the Hacker bypassing security and the Gentleman distracting guards, allows for creative and varied approaches to each mission.

- **Private & Public Lobbies**: You can either join an existing game or create your own private session. In private lobbies, you can invite friends to form your own crew, while public lobbies allow you to meet new players from around the world. The game features matchmaking that ensures you're paired with players of a similar skill level, making multiplayer sessions enjoyable and challenging.

- **Co-Op Strategy**: Communication is key in *Monaco 2*'s multiplayer mode. The game includes built-in voice chat and contextual ping systems, which help players stay coordinated without needing third-party applications. Whether you're signaling your teammate to take out a guard, or coordinating your movements during a tense escape, *Monaco 2* encourages cooperation and teamwork.

## 3. Competitive Multiplayer Mode

In addition to cooperative gameplay, *Monaco 2* introduces a competitive multiplayer mode for those looking to test their skills against other players. This mode allows players to compete in heists, with the goal of outsmarting and outmaneuvering each other rather than working together.

- **PvP Heists**: Players can engage in head-to-head heists where two teams of players compete to complete their objectives first. Each team is tasked with robbing a high-profile target, and the competition comes in the form of who can complete the heist the fastest or with the most finesse. This mode tests your ability to not only execute a perfect heist but also to sabotage your opponents' progress without getting caught.

- **Leaderboards**: In competitive mode, you can track your performance on global leaderboards. Whether you're competing in speed, stealth, or execution quality, the leaderboards offer a way to compare your skills with other players from around the world.

## 4. Custom Game Mode

For those who want to shake things up or create unique challenges, *Monaco 2* includes a custom game mode that allows players to tweak settings and parameters for a more personalized experience.

- **Custom Heist Setup**: In this mode, players can modify various elements of the game, such as enemy AI difficulty, the layout of levels, and the tools available for the heist. This is perfect for players who want to create their own challenges or experiment with different scenarios. You can make heists harder, introduce more security measures, or even add unique twists like restricted abilities.

- **Mission Editor**: For the truly creative players, *Monaco 2* offers a mission editor that allows you to build your own custom levels. You can design your own heists, placing obstacles, guards, objectives, and even traps, and then share them with the community. This brings nearly limitless replayability to the game, as players can enjoy user-created content beyond the base game.

## 5. Cross-Platform Play

*Monaco 2* supports cross-platform play, allowing players from different platforms—whether on PC, PlayStation, Xbox, or Switch—to team up and join the same multiplayer sessions. This feature opens up the player base, making it easier to find matches and ensuring that you can play with your friends regardless of the platform they're on.

- **Seamless Cross-Platform Experience**: Whether you're on a PC or playing on a console, you'll be able to interact with friends and strangers alike, without any barriers. Cross-platform play ensures a thriving multiplayer community and adds variety to the types of players you can encounter.

## 6. Online vs. Local Play

- **Online Play**: Players can connect to online servers and play with others in various multiplayer modes. Online play ensures that you can enjoy *Monaco 2* with friends across the globe, regardless of physical location.

- **Local Play**: For those who prefer a more intimate experience or want to play with friends at home, *Monaco 2* also supports local multiplayer. You can enjoy couch co-op by connecting multiple controllers to your system (available on PlayStation, Xbox, and Switch) and work together to complete the heists. Local play brings a more personal, hands-on experience to the game.

## 7. Future Updates & Additional Modes

The developers have indicated that *Monaco 2* will receive regular updates that will introduce new game modes, heists, and multiplayer options. Whether through seasonal content updates or major expansions, players can look forward to new challenges and content after the game's launch.

# Chapter 2: Getting Started

## 2.1 Installing & Setting Up the Game

Getting *Monaco 2* set up and ready to play is an easy process, whether you're playing on PC or console. Follow the steps below to install the game and set it up for an optimal experience.

### 1. Installing *Monaco 2* on PC

You can install *Monaco 2* on your PC through popular digital distribution platforms like Steam or the Epic Games Store. Here's how to do it:

**Steam Installation**

1. **Purchase the Game**

   - Open **Steam** and search for *Monaco 2* in the store.

   - Add the game to your cart and proceed to checkout to purchase it.

2. **Download and Install**

   - After purchase, go to your **Library**.

   - Click on **Install** next to *Monaco 2*.

   - The game will automatically begin downloading, and Steam will install it on your PC.

3. **Launch the Game**

   ○ Once the download is complete, click **Play** from your **Library** to launch the game.

**Epic Games Store Installation**

1. **Purchase the Game**

   ○ Open the **Epic Games Launcher** and search for *Monaco 2.*

   ○ Add it to your cart and complete the purchase.

2. **Download and Install**

   ○ After purchase, go to your **Library** in the Epic Games Launcher.

   ○ Click **Install** and select the folder where you'd like to install the game.

3. **Launch the Game**

   ○ Once installation is complete, click **Launch** to start playing.

## 2. Installing *Monaco 2* on Consoles

For PlayStation, Xbox, and Nintendo Switch users, *Monaco 2* can be purchased and downloaded directly from the respective digital stores.

### PlayStation (PS4 & PS5)

1. **Purchase the Game**

   o  Navigate to the **PlayStation Store** on your console.

   o  Search for *Monaco 2*, then complete your purchase.

2. **Download and Install**

   o  The game will automatically begin downloading once purchased. Monitor the download from the **Notifications** section.

3. **Launch the Game**

   o  Once downloaded, find the game on your **Home Screen** or **Library**, and press **X** to play.


### Xbox (Xbox One & Xbox Series X|S)

1. **Purchase the Game**

   o  Go to the **Microsoft Store** on your console.

   o  Search for *Monaco 2* and complete your purchase.

2. **Download and Install**

   o  The game will start downloading automatically after your purchase.

- You can check the download progress from **My Games & Apps**.

3. **Launch the Game**

- After installation, select *Monaco 2* from **My Games & Apps** and press **A** to start playing.

**Nintendo Switch**

1. **Purchase the Game**

- Open the **Nintendo eShop** on your Switch.

- Search for *Monaco 2* and complete the purchase.

2. **Download and Install**

- Once purchased, the game will begin downloading automatically.

3. **Launch the Game**

- After the game finishes downloading, select *Monaco 2* from the **Home Menu** and press **A** to play.

# 3. Setting Up the Game

After installing the game, follow these steps to get the best experience out of *Monaco 2*:

### Initial Setup

1. **Adjust Game Settings**
   The first time you launch *Monaco 2*, you'll be prompted to adjust various settings, including graphics, controls, and audio:

   - **Graphics Settings**: Customize resolution, texture quality, and frame rate (for PC players). Consoles automatically set the best graphics settings based on the platform.

   - **Audio Settings**: Adjust sound effects, music, and voice chat volume.

   - **Control Settings**: Customize key bindings or button mapping for your preferred control scheme (keyboard and mouse for PC, controller support for consoles).

2. **Create or Log into an Account**

   - If you plan to play multiplayer, you'll need to log into or create an account on your platform (Steam, Epic Games, PlayStation Network, Xbox Live, or Nintendo Online).

   - This will allow you to save progress, access cross-platform play, and sync data across different devices.

3. **Choose Your Preferred Language and Region**
   *Monaco 2* offers various language options and region-based content. Select your preferred language and ensure your region is set correctly for any location-specific content or

services.

**Configuring Graphics and Performance**

If your system meets the recommended specifications (see section 1.3), the game should run smoothly. However, if you experience any performance issues:

- **PC Users**: You can lower settings like shadow quality, anti-aliasing, and texture resolution for smoother gameplay.

- **Console Users**: The game automatically optimizes performance for your console, but make sure your system is updated to the latest firmware for the best experience.

# 2.2 User Interface & HUD Explanation

The User Interface (UI) and Heads-Up Display (HUD) in *Monaco 2* are designed to provide players with all the critical information needed for heists while maintaining a clean and immersive experience. Whether you're playing solo or with a team, understanding how to interpret the UI and HUD elements is crucial to success. This section breaks down the key components of the game's interface, ensuring you're always in control during a heist.

## 1. Main Menu UI

When you first launch *Monaco 2*, the main menu presents a clean and intuitive interface that allows you to navigate between different game modes, settings, and options.

- **Start Game**: This is where you begin your heist. Selecting this option leads you to the mission selection screen, where you can choose to play the story mode, cooperative multiplayer, or custom missions.

- **Options**: Here you can adjust game settings such as graphics, audio, controls, and accessibility options. It's a good idea to check these settings before starting your first heist.

- **Multiplayer**: This section is dedicated to online and local multiplayer. You can create or join a game with friends or random players. It includes options for public and private lobbies.

- **Extras**: Additional content such as the credits, community creations, and DLCs (Downloadable Content) are accessible here.

- **Exit**: If you're finished or need a break, this option exits the game or takes you back to the desktop.

## 2. In-Game HUD Overview

The HUD in *Monaco 2* provides all the essential information you'll need during gameplay. Whether you're sneaking past guards or cracking safes, the HUD is designed to give you a real-time overview of your progress, environment, and objectives.

### 2.1. Character Information

- **Character Portrait**: At the top left or bottom left of the screen, you'll see the portrait of the character you're currently controlling. This portrait is accompanied by:

○ **Health Bar**: A visual representation of your character's health. If the health bar depletes, your character will be incapacitated and may need to be revived by a teammate in multiplayer.

○ **Special Ability Meter**: Each character in *Monaco 2* has a unique ability (such as hacking or distracting guards). The ability meter shows how much energy is left for these special actions.

## 2.2. Mini-Map

The mini-map, located in the upper-right corner of the screen, is your key navigation tool during the heist. It shows the layout of the current level and important elements such as:

- **Player Position**: Your character is marked by a dot or icon.

- **Objective Markers**: These are shown as icons or symbols on the map, indicating where you need to go or what you need to do (e.g., reach the vault, disable the security system).

- **Guard Positions**: Guards are displayed on the mini-map, helping you avoid detection. Their vision cones or alert status are usually represented by color-coded icons.

- **Exit Points**: These are marked clearly and show the location of escape routes, which are essential for completing the heist and making a clean getaway.

## 2.3. Mission Progress & Objectives

This section is displayed either at the top or bottom of the screen and provides detailed information about your current objectives. It includes:

- **Primary Objective**: The main goal of your current heist (e.g., rob a bank, steal a specific item).

- **Secondary Objectives**: Optional tasks that can give you additional points or rewards (e.g., disable all cameras, steal extra loot).

- **Timer** (if applicable): In time-based missions, this shows how much time remains before the heist becomes more complicated or before the alarm is triggered.

- **Mission Complete Indicator**: When you've completed a task or objective, a checkmark or similar indicator will appear next to it.

## 2.4. Inventory

- **Item Icons**: At the bottom of the screen (or on the side, depending on the platform), you'll see icons representing items in your inventory. These might include tools like lockpicks, grenades, or smoke bombs, as well as any special equipment you've picked up during the mission.

- **Item Count**: Next to each item, you'll see a number representing how many of that item you have left. Keep track of your supplies, as running out of critical tools can jeopardize the success of the heist.

## 2.5. Alerts and Notifications

Throughout the game, certain alerts or notifications will pop up on the screen. These serve to inform you of important events happening in the game:

- **Guard Alerts**: If a guard notices you or hears a noise, a notification will pop up, signaling that they're investigating your location or are aware of your presence.

- **Objective Updates**: As you progress through the mission, the HUD will update with new objective information or changes.

- **Damage Taken**: If you take damage, a red flash on the screen or a warning icon may appear. This is your cue to heal or find cover.

## 2.6. Player Communication (Multiplayer)

In multiplayer mode, the HUD includes communication options for coordinating with teammates:

- **Voice Chat Indicator**: If you're using voice chat, an icon will appear showing who is speaking.

- **Ping System**: Players can use a contextual ping system to indicate specific areas of interest (e.g., "Look out for guards here" or "Here's where the loot is").

- **Teammate Health**: You can see the health status of your teammates, which is crucial for rescuing downed players or coordinating healing.

## 3. Navigating the World

- **Interactive Objects**: Items that can be interacted with (e.g., doors, security systems, safes) are highlighted when you approach them. These objects are typically shown with a glowing effect or a contextual button prompt (e.g., "Press E to Hack" or "Hold X to Open Door").

- **Stealth Indicators**: In stealth sections, your HUD will provide visual cues like an eye icon or a sound meter, indicating whether you're visible or making noise. This helps you gauge whether you're about to be detected by enemies.

## 4. Customizing the HUD

*Monaco 2* provides the ability to adjust the HUD elements for a more personalized experience. In the **Options** menu, you can:

- **Toggle or adjust visibility** for certain HUD elements (e.g., mini-map, objective markers, etc.).

- **Adjust the size** of the HUD elements if you prefer a more minimalistic interface or if you have accessibility needs.

- **Enable colorblind mode** for better visibility of certain indicators like enemy vision cones or objective markers.

# 2.3 Controls & Customization Options

In *Monaco 2*, mastering the controls is essential for executing successful heists. Whether you're sneaking past guards, hacking systems, or escaping with the loot, understanding and customizing the controls will help you perform better. This section will break down the default control scheme and guide you through the customization options to tailor your gameplay experience.

# 1. Default Control Scheme

### 1.1. PC Controls

On PC, *Monaco 2* supports both keyboard and mouse as well as gamepad input. Below is the default control setup for each.

**Keyboard and Mouse:**

- **W, A, S, D**: Move character (up, left, down, right)

- **Mouse**: Aim and look around

    - **Left Mouse Button**: Interact with objects, pick up items, or attack (if applicable)

    - **Right Mouse Button**: Use the character's special ability

- **E**: Use an item or interact with objects (e.g., hack a terminal, open a door)

- **Q**: Drop item (e.g., throw a grenade or place an item)

- **F**: Focus/zoom in (for better precision when aiming or hacking)

- **R**: Reload weapon (if applicable)

- **Spacebar**: Sprint (if available for the character)

- **Shift (Hold)**: Crouch (for stealth)

- **Tab**: Open the map or objectives list

- **Esc**: Pause the game or open the main menu

- **1-4 (Number Keys)**: Select items in your inventory (e.g., lockpicks, smoke bombs, etc.)

**Gamepad Controls (for Xbox/PlayStation controllers on PC)**

- **Left Stick**: Move character (up, down, left, right)

- **Right Stick**: Aim and look around

- **A (Xbox) / X (PlayStation)**: Interact with objects, pick up items, or attack

- **B (Xbox) / Circle (PlayStation)**: Use character's special ability

- **X (Xbox) / Square (PlayStation)**: Use an item or interact with objects

- **LT (Xbox) / L2 (PlayStation)**: Crouch (for stealth)

- **RT (Xbox) / R2 (PlayStation)**: Sprint (if available)

- **Y (Xbox) / Triangle (PlayStation)**: Drop item (e.g., throw a grenade or place an item)

- **Start**: Open the main menu or pause the game

- **Back (Xbox) / Select (PlayStation)**: Open inventory or map

## 1.2. Console Controls

The default control schemes for *Monaco 2* on consoles (PlayStation, Xbox, and Nintendo Switch) are similar to those of PC but adjusted for each console's respective controllers. Here's a brief breakdown:

**PlayStation (PS4/PS5)**

- **Left Stick**: Move character

- **Right Stick**: Aim and look around

- **Square**: Interact or pick up objects

- **Circle**: Use special ability

- **X**: Drop item or interact with the environment

- **R2**: Sprint (when available)

- **L2**: Crouch (for stealth)

- **L1**: Switch items in the inventory

- **Start**: Open the main menu or pause

- **Touchpad**: Open map or objectives

- **Options**: Inventory

**Xbox (Xbox One/Xbox Series X|S)**

- **Left Stick**: Move character

- **Right Stick**: Aim and look around

- **A**: Interact or pick up objects

- **B**: Use special ability

- **X**: Drop item or interact with the environment

- **RT**: Sprint

- **LT**: Crouch (for stealth)

- **RB**: Switch items in the inventory

- **Menu**: Open the main menu or pause

- **View**: Open map or objectives

**Nintendo Switch**

- **Left Stick**: Move character

- **Right Stick**: Aim and look around

- **A**: Interact or pick up objects

- **B**: Use special ability

- **X**: Drop item or interact with the environment

- **R**: Sprint

- **L**: Crouch (for stealth)

- **ZL/ZR**: Switch items in the inventory

- **Start**: Open main menu or pause

- **Plus Button**: Open map or objectives

## 2. Customizing Controls

Customizing the controls can provide a more personalized gameplay experience. Here's how you can customize your controls in *Monaco 2* to fit your playstyle:

### 2.1. Key Binding (PC)

On PC, you can change your key bindings for a more comfortable setup. To customize your controls:

1. **Access the Options Menu**: From the main menu, go to **Options** and select **Controls**.

2. **Adjust Key Bindings**: The game will present you with a list of all actions and their corresponding key bindings.

   - Click on any action (e.g., **Interact, Use Ability, Sprint**) and press the new key you want to assign.

o   You can rebind any key for your convenience. For example, if you prefer **F** for sprinting instead of **Shift**, just assign it in the settings.

3. **Save Settings**: Once you're happy with your changes, save the settings and return to the game.

### 2.2. Gamepad Configuration (PC & Consoles)

On consoles, the controls are preset, but on PC, you can also adjust or switch between different controller layouts. If you're using a gamepad, here's how to configure it:

1. **Access the Options Menu**: From the main menu, go to **Options** and select **Controls**.

2. **Controller Layouts**: You can choose between different layouts or even remap buttons for your controller.

3. **Custom Profiles**: On certain platforms like Steam, you can save custom controller profiles to switch between different control schemes quickly.

### 2.3. Adjusting Sensitivity

You may want to adjust the sensitivity of your mouse or gamepad to ensure smooth and precise aiming. This is especially useful for stealth-heavy gameplay where subtle movements are important.

1. **Mouse Sensitivity (PC)**: In the **Controls** settings menu, look for the **Mouse Sensitivity** slider. Increase or decrease the sensitivity based on your preference.

2. **Gamepad Sensitivity**: Similarly, gamepad users can adjust the **Aim Sensitivity** and **Movement Sensitivity** in the settings menu to make the controls feel more responsive or easier to control.

### 2.4. Accessibility Options

*Monaco 2* includes several accessibility options to make the game more enjoyable for everyone. These options can be found in the **Options** menu under **Accessibility**:

- **Subtitles**: Turn on subtitles for in-game dialogue.

- **Colorblind Mode**: Adjust color settings to make the HUD more readable for players with colorblindness.

- **Visual Cues**: Enable or adjust visual cues for actions like low health, detecting guards, or mission objectives.

## 3. Tips for Mastering Controls

- **Practice in Training Mode**: Before diving into missions, spend some time in a non-combat area to practice your movements and interactions with the environment.

- **Switch to a Gamepad**: If you're playing on PC and prefer a controller, using a gamepad may provide a smoother experience during multiplayer sessions.

- **Use Hotkeys for Quick Actions**: If you're using a keyboard and mouse, assign frequently used items or abilities to the number keys for quicker access during heists.

- **Stay Consistent**: Once you've found a control layout you're comfortable with, try to stick to it to build muscle memory, especially for more complex missions.

# 2.4 Basic Mechanics & Movement

In *Monaco 2*, mastering the basic mechanics and movement is essential for surviving and succeeding in your heists. Whether you're sneaking past guards, escaping through tight spaces, or using your environment to your advantage, understanding these mechanics will give you the edge in every mission. This section covers the core movement system and gameplay mechanics to help you perform the most precise and efficient actions.

## 1. Basic Movement

Moving your character around is the foundation of all heists. In *Monaco 2*, your movement needs to be strategic, quick, and stealthy.

### 1.1. Walking and Running

- **Walking**: You will move at a moderate pace by default. Walking is useful when you need to move quietly or when you're near guards or other enemies. It's important to stay as silent as possible to avoid detection.

- **Running**: To move faster, use the **Sprint** command:

  - **PC**: Hold **Shift** (default)

  - **Gamepad**: Hold **RT (Xbox) / R2 (PlayStation) / R (Switch)**.

Running is useful for covering distance quickly but can alert guards to your presence if you're not careful. Use it wisely in areas where you know you're safe or during escapes.

## 1.2. Crouching

Crouching is an important stealth mechanic in *Monaco 2*. When you crouch, your character will move slower but make less noise, making it easier to avoid detection by enemies.

- **PC**: Press **Ctrl** or hold **Shift** while moving for crouch-walking.

- **Gamepad**: Hold **LT (Xbox/PlayStation)** or **L (Switch)** to crouch.

Use crouching when navigating near guards, or to stay hidden in the shadows. This is critical for stealth missions and escaping enemy sight.

## 1.3. Interacting with the Environment

Your environment is a key part of your movement. Interacting with doors, windows, or other objects can be the difference between success and failure.

- **PC**: Press **E** to interact with objects like doors, hack terminals, pick locks, or trigger other events in the environment.

- **Gamepad**: Press **X** (Xbox/PlayStation) or **A (Switch)** to interact with objects.

Understanding when and how to interact with the environment efficiently is key to planning successful heists.

## 2. Advanced Movement

In addition to basic walking, running, and crouching, *Monaco 2* allows for more advanced movement techniques to help you navigate the map and deal with obstacles.

### 2.1. Vaulting and Climbing

Certain obstacles in the environment, such as low walls, railings, or other vertical surfaces, can be overcome by vaulting or climbing.

- **PC**: Approach the object and press **Spacebar** to vault over it. For climbing ladders or similar surfaces, use **W** to climb.

- **Gamepad**: Approach the obstacle and press **A** (Xbox/PlayStation) or **B (Switch)** to vault over it.

Vaulting is especially useful when evading enemies or quickly traversing areas, while climbing can help you reach higher ground for strategic advantages.

### 2.2. Rolling and Sliding

When evading detection or needing to move quickly through tight spaces, rolling or sliding can give you an extra burst of speed.

- **PC**: Press **Q** or double-tap **W** (depending on your configuration) for a roll or slide action.

- **Gamepad**: Press **B** (Xbox/PlayStation) or **Circle (Switch)** to roll or slide.

Use this mechanic to quickly escape a close encounter or to dive under a low barrier without losing momentum.

## 3. Stealth & Noise Mechanics

In *Monaco 2*, stealth is vital. Many of your missions will require you to move undetected, and this involves managing your noise and visibility.

### 3.1. Noise Level

Every action you take generates a certain amount of noise, which can alert nearby guards. Activities like sprinting, opening doors, or breaking glass are more likely to make noise. To avoid detection, try the following:

- **Walk, don't run**: Running generates more noise, while walking keeps you stealthier.

- **Use cover**: Stay behind objects like walls, pillars, and furniture to reduce the risk of being seen.

- **Distracting Guards**: Use objects to create distractions, drawing guards away from your path, giving you the opportunity to move safely.

### 3.2. Guard Vision & Awareness

Guards in *Monaco 2* are equipped with a cone of vision that they use to detect your presence. Moving in their line of sight or making too much noise will increase your chances of being caught.

- **Guard Vision Cone**: Pay attention to the visual indicators of guards. Their cone of vision is represented on the map and by visual cues. If you're seen, the alert level will increase.

- **Alert Status**: If a guard hears a noise or spots you, they will go into an "alerted" state and search for you. If they catch sight of you, the mission could be compromised.

Stealth is about patience, so make sure to keep an eye on guard movements and avoid their vision cones.

## 4. Special Movement Abilities

Each character in *Monaco 2* has a special ability related to movement. Understanding these abilities can help you make more efficient moves during a heist.

### 4.1. Unique Character Abilities

Each character has their own unique movement mechanic that adds a layer of strategy to their role in the heist.

- **The Hacker**: The hacker can bypass security systems more efficiently, and they have a special movement ability that allows them to move through restricted areas unnoticed for a short time.

- **The Pickpocket**: The pickpocket has the ability to run faster and jump over obstacles more quickly, which helps them evade capture during intense moments.

- **The Cleaner**: The cleaner can move quietly and is faster when crouching, making them perfect for stealth-focused missions.

Using these abilities at the right moment can change the course of a mission and help you reach your goal faster.

## 5. Interacting with Objects & Environment

While movement is essential, interacting with your environment is equally important. These interactions can help you gain advantages, escape danger, or solve puzzles.

### 5.1. Opening & Closing Doors

In *Monaco 2*, doors are a primary way to navigate between areas, but they can also be a source of danger if you're not careful.

- **Opening Doors**: When approaching a door, press **E** (PC) or **X** (Gamepad) to open it. Be aware that opening doors too quickly or too loudly can alert nearby guards.

- **Closing Doors**: After entering an area, you can close doors behind you to help block guards or make it more difficult for them to follow you.

### 5.2. Hiding and Concealment

In certain environments, there are places you can hide to avoid detection by guards.

- **Hiding in Shadows**: Look for dark areas or places where you can crouch to blend in with the environment.

- **Hiding Objects**: You can also hide behind or inside certain objects (like crates, cabinets, or lockers), which is useful if guards are approaching.

### 5.3. Using the Environment for Advantage

Sometimes, you may encounter things like security cameras, alarms, or traps. Knowing how to disable or avoid these environmental obstacles can be crucial.

- **Disabling Security Systems**: Certain characters have the ability to disable security cameras, alarms, or other surveillance equipment. The **Hacker** is especially useful here.

- **Using Environmental Objects**: You can use items like smoke bombs, fire extinguishers, or explosives to clear paths or distract enemies, giving you the upper hand during a heist.

## 6. Mastering Movement for Heist Success

- **Use Cover**: Always look for objects or walls that you can hide behind to avoid being detected by enemies.

- **Take It Slow**: In stealth-heavy missions, taking your time to move carefully will often yield better results than rushing.

- **Coordinate with Teammates**: In multiplayer, use advanced movement techniques and abilities to support each other. For example, one player can create a distraction while others move through restricted areas.

# Chapter 3: The Crew & Characters

## 3.1 Character Classes & Their Roles

In *Monaco 2*, each character is designed with a unique role and set of skills that contribute to the success of your heist. Understanding the strengths and roles of each character is key to executing a well-planned and efficient operation. Below are the primary character classes and their roles within the game:

### 1. The Hacker (Tech Specialist)

- **Role**: The Hacker is a master of technology and systems. Their role is to disable security systems, hack terminals, and manipulate electronic devices to give the team an advantage.

- **Strengths**: Excellent at bypassing security systems, including cameras, alarms, and locked doors. They can also access computer terminals to gather intel or disable enemy detection.

- **Weaknesses**: The Hacker has lower physical stats (health, stamina) compared to other characters, so they must rely on stealth and technology to stay safe.

### 2. The Pickpocket (Stealth Expert)

- **Role**: The Pickpocket is a stealthy and nimble character, capable of slipping past guards unnoticed and stealing items without being detected.

- **Strengths**: High mobility and stealth. They can steal items from enemies or interact with the environment without raising alarms. The Pickpocket can also move quickly through the map, making them great for sneaky missions.

- **Weaknesses**: Lacks heavy combat skills, making them vulnerable in direct confrontations. Best used in stealthy, tactical playstyles.

### 3. The Cleaner (Combat Specialist)

- **Role**: The Cleaner is the team's go-to for handling dangerous situations. They excel in combat and can handle large groups of enemies.

- **Strengths**: High combat ability, capable of taking down enemies quickly with either firearms or close-quarters combat. The Cleaner also has excellent health and stamina, making them resilient in high-stress situations.

- **Weaknesses**: Less stealthy and more noticeable, so the Cleaner is not as suited for missions requiring discretion or subtlety.

### 4. The Gentleman (Social Engineer)

- **Role**: The Gentleman is a master of persuasion and diplomacy, able to manipulate NPCs, distract enemies, or charm their way through obstacles.

- **Strengths**: Excellent at distracting guards, convincing NPCs to help, or gaining access to restricted areas without confrontation. The Gentleman can also defuse hostile situations with their charisma.

- **Weaknesses**: Weak in direct combat situations. Their primary strength lies in social interactions and clever manipulation rather than physical confrontation.

## 5. The Mole (Demolition Expert)

- **Role**: The Mole specializes in using explosives and creating tactical advantages through destruction. They're great for clearing paths and dealing with enemy fortifications.

- **Strengths**: High explosive damage, great for breaching locked areas or creating distractions. The Mole can cause significant chaos during missions, clearing space or taking out high-security areas.

- **Weaknesses**: Explosives can sometimes be unpredictable, requiring precise planning to avoid harming the team or alerting enemies prematurely.

# 3.2 Unique Abilities & Strengths

Each character in *Monaco 2* comes equipped with a unique ability that sets them apart from the rest. Understanding how to leverage these abilities during missions will enhance your chances of success.

# 1. The Hacker: System Override

- **Ability**: The Hacker can temporarily disable security systems, including cameras, alarms, and locked doors, creating safe routes for the team.

- **Usefulness**: This ability is invaluable when navigating high-security areas, allowing other team members to pass unnoticed. The Hacker is essential for eliminating electronic surveillance.

# 2. The Pickpocket: Quick Fingers

- **Ability**: The Pickpocket can steal items from NPCs and enemies without being detected, even when in close proximity.

- **Usefulness**: This ability is great for acquiring key items, such as money, keys, or critical tools, that are essential for completing objectives without alerting enemies.

# 3. The Cleaner: Heavy Hands

- **Ability**: The Cleaner can overpower enemies in hand-to-hand combat, dealing high damage to enemies and incapacitating them swiftly.

- **Usefulness**: The Cleaner is the best choice for situations where stealth is no longer an option. Their combat proficiency makes them ideal for defending the team or clearing a path when necessary.

### 4. The Gentleman: Persuasion

- **Ability**: The Gentleman can charm and distract enemies or NPCs, causing them to ignore the player or give helpful information.

- **Usefulness**: This ability is especially useful when trying to avoid combat or gain access to restricted areas without raising suspicion. The Gentleman's charm can turn hostile NPCs into allies.

### 5. The Mole: Explosive Entry

- **Ability**: The Mole can plant explosives to break through locked doors, walls, or enemy fortifications, opening up new pathways or causing chaos.

- **Usefulness**: This ability is best used in situations where stealth isn't a priority, and a loud distraction is necessary. The Mole is also a great tool for clearing obstacles that may be blocking the team's progress.

## 3.3 Best Character Combinations for Teams

In *Monaco 2*, teamwork is essential, and selecting the right combination of characters can make or break your heist. Below are a few recommended character combinations based on mission type and playstyle:

# 1. Stealth & Precision Team

- **Recommended Characters**: The Hacker, The Pickpocket, and The Gentleman.

- **Strengths**: This team excels in stealth, allowing for smooth operations without raising alarms. The Hacker disables security systems, while the Pickpocket gathers intel and the Gentleman charms enemies. This team is perfect for infiltrating high-security areas quietly.

- **Weaknesses**: This team lacks direct combat power, so if stealth is compromised, they may struggle.

# 2. Combat-Heavy Team

- **Recommended Characters**: The Cleaner, The Mole, and The Hacker.

- **Strengths**: This team is balanced with heavy combat skills and technical prowess. The Cleaner handles enemies directly, the Mole creates tactical breaches, and the Hacker disables electronic security. This setup is ideal for missions requiring aggressive play and tactical destruction.

- **Weaknesses**: The team's lack of stealth abilities means they may struggle in missions that require precision and subtlety.

### 3. Balanced Team

- **Recommended Characters**: The Hacker, The Cleaner, and The Pickpocket.

- **Strengths**: A well-rounded team, combining tech, combat, and stealth. The Hacker can disable security, the Cleaner handles combat situations, and the Pickpocket gathers useful items without detection. This team can adapt to various mission types.

- **Weaknesses**: The team lacks some specialized abilities like those of the Gentleman or Mole, but it's still very versatile for most situations.

## 3.4 Unlocking New Characters

As you progress through *Monaco 2*, you'll have the opportunity to unlock additional characters with unique abilities and skills. These new characters provide fresh playstyles and options, making each mission more dynamic.

### 1. How to Unlock New Characters

- **Story Progression**: New characters may become available as you progress through the game's story or complete specific chapters. Each new character is unlocked after you reach a particular milestone or complete a specific mission.

- **Challenges & Achievements**: Some characters may be unlocked by completing certain in-game challenges or achievements. These can include tasks like stealthy escapes, successful combat sequences, or completing missions without triggering alarms.

- **Special Events or DLC**: Certain characters may be introduced through special in-game events or downloadable content (DLC). Keep an eye on updates to unlock exclusive characters.

- **Unlocking via Multiplayer**: In multiplayer mode, some characters are unlocked through team achievements or by completing group objectives. Collaborating with others can unlock powerful characters that are difficult to obtain solo.

## 2. Tips for Unlocking Characters

- **Focus on Stealth**: If you prefer stealthy characters, focus on completing missions without alerting guards. Many stealth-focused characters are unlocked through stealth achievements.

- **Complete Side Missions**: Some side missions offer unlockable characters upon completion. Take the time to tackle these objectives for additional rewards.

- **Experiment with Different Playstyles**: Try out different characters during multiplayer sessions to see which ones fit your playstyle. This can help you decide which character to focus on unlocking next.

# Chapter 4: Heist Planning & Strategy

## 4.1 Understanding Level Layouts & Objectives

Every mission in *Monaco 2* is set within a carefully designed level, each with its own challenges, objectives, and opportunities for creative solutions. Understanding how these levels are structured and what you need to accomplish is key to executing a successful heist.

### 1. Level Layouts & Exploration

- **Multi-Layered Maps** – Most levels are designed with multiple floors, hidden passages, and various entry/exit points. Exploring your surroundings before committing to a strategy is crucial.

- **Alternative Routes** – Some areas have multiple ways to reach objectives, including ventilation shafts, locked doors, or destructible walls. Identify the best route based on your team composition.

- **Restricted Areas & Guard Patrols** – Many locations have high-security zones that require stealth or distraction tactics to navigate without raising an alarm.

## 2. Common Objectives in Heist Missions

Your main objectives in *Monaco 2* will vary from mission to mission, but most fall into one of the following categories:

- **Steal Valuable Items** – Retrieve important loot, such as cash, gems, or critical documents.

- **Hack Security Systems** – Disable alarms, cameras, or electronic locks to make movement safer.

- **Rescue or Extract VIPs** – Some missions involve breaking out a prisoner or escorting a character to safety.

- **Escape Without Detection** – In high-security heists, the goal is often to leave without alerting guards or triggering alarms.

By carefully analyzing the level layout and understanding your objectives before making a move, you'll significantly improve your chances of success.

# 4.2 The Importance of Stealth vs Action

Deciding whether to take a stealthy approach or engage in direct action can determine the outcome of a mission. While some situations may require quick reflexes and combat skills, most heists reward patience and careful planning.

# 1. The Benefits of Stealth

- **Avoiding Alarms** – Staying undetected prevents reinforcements from arriving, keeping security levels low.

- **More Reward, Less Risk** – Many missions provide bonuses for completing objectives without getting caught.

- **Silent Takedowns** – Using stealth takedowns, hiding in the shadows, and staying out of sight can clear obstacles without raising suspicion.

**Best Characters for Stealth:** *The Pickpocket, The Hacker, The Gentleman*

# 2. When to Go Loud (Action-Based Approach)

- **If You're Discovered** – Sometimes, even the best plans fail. If an alarm is triggered, you might need to fight your way out.

- **High-Security Areas** – Some objectives require force, such as breaking open a vault or eliminating threats.

- **Distraction Tactics** – A controlled "loud" approach can sometimes serve as a distraction while teammates complete objectives elsewhere.

**Best Characters for Combat:** *The Cleaner, The Mole*

### 3. Balancing Both Playstyles

- **Start with Stealth, Switch to Action When Necessary** – If you can complete objectives quietly, do so. But be prepared for action if things go south.

- **Use the Right Team** – A mix of stealth-focused and combat-ready characters allows for flexibility.

- **Have an Escape Plan** – Always know where the exits are in case an alarm is triggered.

The best teams know when to be ghosts and when to be brawlers. A well-balanced approach will help you navigate any mission.

# 4.3 Choosing the Right Tools & Gear

Selecting the right tools and equipment for a mission can give you a tactical edge. Every character has access to different gear, and knowing which ones to bring can make or break a heist.

### 1. Essential Tools for Heists

- **Lockpicks** – Used to silently open locked doors and safes without attracting attention.

- **Hacking Devices** – The Hacker's specialty, these disable cameras, alarms, and security doors.

- **Smoke Bombs** – Provide cover to escape or move past guards unnoticed.

- **Explosives** – The Mole can use these to create new entrances or take out groups of enemies.

- **Disguises** – The Gentleman can use disguises to blend in and walk past enemies undetected.

## 2. Weaponry & Defensive Equipment

While *Monaco 2* is heavily focused on stealth, sometimes combat is unavoidable. Some weapons and gear options include:

- **Tranquilizer Darts** – Silently take down enemies without killing them.

- **Silenced Pistols** – Small, quiet firearms for emergency situations.

- **Melee Weapons** – The Cleaner specializes in hand-to-hand combat, making melee weapons highly effective.

- **Armor & Medkits** – If combat is expected, extra armor or healing items can keep you alive longer.

## 3. How to Choose the Right Gear

- **If Going Stealthy:** Focus on lockpicks, hacking devices, and smoke bombs.

- **If Expecting Combat:** Bring silencers, melee weapons, and healing items.

- **If Playing as a Team:** Coordinate your loadouts so each player covers different aspects of the mission.

Smart gear choices make a huge difference in how a mission unfolds, so plan wisely.

# 4.4 Teamwork and Communication

Since *Monaco 2* can be played solo or in multiplayer co-op, teamwork is an essential part of success. Proper communication and coordination with teammates will improve your chances of pulling off the perfect heist.

## 1. Assigning Roles Based on Strengths

Each character excels in different areas, so assign tasks accordingly:

- **The Hacker** – Handles security systems and ensures safe passage.

- **The Pickpocket** – Collects valuable items and stays undetected.

- **The Cleaner** – Deals with enemy threats and clears paths.

- **The Gentleman** – Uses disguises and distractions to help teammates move freely.

- **The Mole** – Creates new paths and breaks through barriers.

A well-balanced team ensures that every aspect of a heist is covered efficiently.

## 2. Coordinating Actions in Multiplayer

- **Use Voice or Text Chat** – Communicate about guard locations, security systems, and enemy movements in real-time.

- **Plan the Escape Route in Advance** – Have a designated meeting point in case things go wrong.

- **Time Actions Carefully** – If one player distracts a guard, another can sneak past. Synchronized actions make heists smoother.

## 3. Adapting to Unexpected Situations

Even the best plans can go wrong. When this happens:

- **Stay Calm** – Don't panic if the alarm is triggered. React strategically.

- **Change the Plan** – If stealth is no longer an option, shift to a new strategy.

- **Cover for Each Other** – If a teammate is caught, others can create distractions or rescue them.

# Chapter 5: The Heists – Mission Breakdown

## 5.1 Introduction to Heists & Objectives

Heists are the core gameplay experience in *Monaco 2*, requiring a mix of strategy, teamwork, and quick thinking. Each mission presents unique challenges, objectives, and security measures, demanding different approaches based on the team's composition and playstyle.

### 1. The Core Elements of a Heist

Every heist follows a general structure, consisting of:

- **Infiltration** – Getting inside the target location without alerting security.

- **Execution** – Completing the main objective, whether it's stealing an item, hacking a system, or rescuing someone.

- **Escape** – Evacuating the area without being caught by guards or triggering alarms.

### 2. Types of Objectives in Heists

- **Stealing High-Value Targets** – Some missions involve stealing artifacts, money, or confidential data.

- **Hacking & Disabling Security** – The Hacker plays a key role in missions requiring electronic interference.

- **Rescue & Extraction Missions** – Some heists involve freeing hostages or escorting key characters.

- **Sabotage Operations** – Certain missions require destroying key assets or disabling enemy infrastructure.

Before starting a heist, assessing the layout, potential threats, and necessary tools will significantly increase your odds of success.

# 5.2 Mission Walkthroughs – Beginner Heists

These heists serve as an introduction to the game's mechanics, helping players learn the fundamentals of stealth, movement, and teamwork.

## 1. The Jewelry Store Job

- **Objective:** Steal the rare diamond from the main vault.

- **Recommended Characters:** The Hacker (disable alarms), The Pickpocket (grab loot quickly), The Cleaner (neutralize guards if needed).

- **Best Strategy:**

    o   Use **The Hacker** to disable the security system.

- The **Pickpocket** sneaks in through ventilation shafts to grab small valuables along the way.

- The **Cleaner** watches for roaming guards and incapacitates them silently if necessary.

- Escape via the back alley exit to avoid detection.

## 2. The Bank Heist

- **Objective:** Break into the vault and steal stacks of cash.

- **Recommended Characters:** The Mole (create alternative routes), The Gentleman (disguise for deception).

- **Best Strategy:**

  - Use **The Mole** to create shortcuts through walls, bypassing heavy security areas.

  - **The Gentleman** blends in with employees, gaining access to restricted zones.

  - Avoid triggering metal detectors and use smoke bombs if things go wrong.

  - Escape through the underground tunnels.

# 5.3 Mission Walkthroughs – Intermediate Heists

Once you're comfortable with the basics, these heists introduce more complex layouts, multiple objectives, and tougher security.

## 1. The Art Museum Raid

- **Objective:** Steal a priceless painting without setting off motion detectors.

- **Recommended Characters:** The Hacker (disable motion sensors), The Pickpocket (steal smaller artifacts), The Gentleman (social engineering).

- **Best Strategy:**

    - Use **The Hacker** to temporarily disable security cameras and sensors.

    - **The Pickpocket** collects smaller valuables while remaining unseen.

    - **The Gentleman** can create distractions by talking to security guards.

    - Exit through a side window or backdoor before security resets.

### 2. The Underground Casino Heist

- **Objective:** Crack the safe and escape without triggering the silent alarm.

- **Recommended Characters:** The Cleaner (for quick takedowns), The Mole (to bypass locked doors).

- **Best Strategy:**

    - Have **The Cleaner** clear the first floor guards quietly.

    - **The Mole** breaks through a weak wall near the vault, bypassing laser grids.

    - Avoid looting everything at once—some items are rigged with alarms.

    - Once the money is secured, leave through the elevator shaft.

## 5.4 Mission Walkthroughs – Advanced Heists

These high-stakes missions feature the most complex layouts, elite security forces, and multiple objectives that must be completed within tight timeframes.

# 1. The Corporate Tower Break-In

- **Objective:** Hack a high-security server and steal classified data.

- **Recommended Characters:** The Hacker (disable defenses), The Cleaner (combat backup), The Pickpocket (grab keycards).

- **Best Strategy:**

    - **The Hacker** gains access to the building's systems, disabling electronic locks.

    - **The Pickpocket** steals access codes from security personnel.

    - **The Cleaner** eliminates any guards standing in the way.

    - Escape via the rooftop using a zipline to avoid police reinforcements.

# 2. The Grand Vault Heist

- **Objective:** Crack the most secure vault in *Monaco 2*, steal the fortune, and survive an elite SWAT response.

- **Recommended Characters:** The Mole (for demolitions), The Gentleman (for distractions), The Cleaner (for combat).

- **Best Strategy:**

- The **Mole** creates a hidden entry point using explosives.

- The **Gentleman** mingles with VIPs to avoid suspicion.

- Once the vault is open, **The Cleaner** handles enemy resistance as you escape.

- A secondary exit strategy is crucial—police reinforcements arrive quickly.

These advanced heists test your team's ability to adapt under pressure, combining stealth and combat as needed.

# Chapter 6: Tools, Gadgets, and Equipment

## 6.1 Basic Tools for Heists

Tools are essential for executing a smooth heist, allowing players to bypass security, open locked doors, distract guards, or create new escape routes.

### 1. Essential Tools & Their Functions

- **Lockpick** – Quickly unlocks doors and safes without alerting guards. A must-have for stealth-focused characters.

- **Crowbar** – Breaks open doors, crates, and weak walls but is noisier than a lockpick.

- **Hacking Device** – Used to disable security systems like cameras, alarms, and electronic locks.

- **Disguise Kit** – Temporarily lets you blend in with guards or civilians to access restricted areas.

- **Smoke Bombs** – Creates a temporary blind spot, allowing players to evade detection or make a quick getaway.

- **EMP Grenade** – Disables all electronic devices in a radius, shutting down alarms, cameras, and lights for a limited time.

# 6.2 Advanced Gadgets & Their Uses

As you progress in *Monaco 2*, advanced gadgets become available, offering even more ways to manipulate the environment and complete objectives efficiently.

## 1. Specialized Heist Equipment

- **Glass Cutter** – Allows silent entry through windows without breaking them, perfect for high-rise or museum heists.

- **Grappling Hook** – Enables climbing to otherwise inaccessible areas, useful for rooftop escapes.

- **Decoy Device** – Projects fake movement or sounds to mislead guards, creating opportunities to slip past unnoticed.

- **Explosives** – Can blow open doors, safes, and walls but generates noise, attracting enemies. Ideal for aggressive heists.

- **Tranquilizer Dart Gun** – Knocks out guards silently from a distance without killing them, great for stealth runs.

- **Night Vision Goggles** – Allows better visibility in dark areas, helping navigate unlit tunnels or security-restricted zones.

# 6.3 How to Upgrade and Equip Tools

Upgrading your tools enhances their effectiveness, reducing cooldowns, increasing their range, or adding extra features.

# 1. How to Unlock Upgrades

- **Complete Missions** – Some tools upgrade automatically as you progress through the campaign.

- **Spend Heist Earnings** – Use the money earned from successful jobs to buy better gear.

- **Character Progression** – Certain upgrades are tied to specific characters leveling up.

- **Hidden Blueprints** – Some levels contain special blueprints that unlock exclusive tool enhancements.

# 2. Examples of Tool Upgrades

- **Lockpick+** – Reduces the time needed to pick locks.

- **EMP Enhanced** – Extends the duration of electronic shutdowns.

- **Explosive Charges** – Provides a remote detonation option instead of instant blasts.

- **Smoke Bomb 2.0** – Releases a wider smoke cloud and lasts longer.

# 6.4 The Importance of Choosing the Right Gear

Your loadout should complement your team's strengths and the mission objectives.

## 1. Matching Tools to Playstyle

- **Stealth Approach** – Lockpick, hacking device, tranquilizer darts, and disguises are the best options.

- **Aggressive Approach** – Explosives, crowbars, and firearms are ideal for breaking through resistance.

- **Hybrid Approach** – A mix of silent tools (smoke bombs, hacking devices) and defensive tools (decoys, EMP grenades) helps adapt to unexpected situations.

## 2. Coordinating With Teammates

In multiplayer, balancing your team's tools is crucial. For example:

- One player brings hacking tools for electronic security.

- Another carries smoke bombs and decoys for distractions.

- A third player focuses on brute-force entry with explosives or crowbars.

A well-equipped team can handle any heist smoothly and efficiently.

# Chapter 7: Advanced Tactics & Techniques

## 7.1 Mastering Stealth and Distraction

Stealth is the key to a successful heist in *Monaco 2*. Staying undetected allows for smooth execution and a higher success rate.

### 1. Core Stealth Mechanics

- **Line of Sight** – Stay out of guard and camera vision cones. Use cover and shadows to remain hidden.

- **Noise Awareness** – Running, breaking doors, or using weapons generates sound. Move cautiously to avoid drawing attention.

- **Hiding Spots** – Use lockers, bushes, or vents to remain unseen when a threat is nearby.

### 2. Effective Distraction Techniques

- **Decoy Devices** – Use sound-producing tools to lure guards away from key locations.

- **Triggering Alarms Strategically** – Sometimes, setting off a minor alarm can divert guards while your team moves in.

- **Using NPCs & Crowds** – Certain levels have civilians who can be manipulated or used as cover.

Stealth is all about patience and planning rushing in will get you caught.

# 7.2 Combat and Offensive Strategies

While *Monaco 2* is designed around stealth, sometimes combat is unavoidable.

## 1. Understanding Enemy Threats

- **Basic Guards** – Armed with batons or basic firearms, they react to noise and suspicious movement.

- **Elite Security** – More aggressive and better armed, often equipped with armor.

- **SWAT Teams** – Appear in high-alert situations, heavily armed, and difficult to take down.

## 2. Best Combat Tools & Weapons

- **Tranquilizer Darts** – Ideal for silent takedowns without raising an alarm.

- **Melee Attacks** – The Cleaner can neutralize enemies with close-range knockouts.

- **Firearms** – Useful for emergencies but extremely loud, alerting reinforcements.

- **Explosives** – Good for clearing rooms or creating escape routes but attract a lot of attention.

### 3. Combat vs. Stealth – When to Fight

- **Only Engage If Necessary** – Combat should be a last resort when escape is impossible.

- **Use Cover & Hit Fast** – If fighting is required, use walls and objects to stay out of direct fire.

- **Know When to Retreat** – If overwhelmed, escape and regroup instead of forcing a losing battle.

A well-balanced team should always have an exit strategy in case things turn violent.

# 7.3 Avoiding Detection & Escaping Safely

Even the best heists go wrong sometimes—knowing how to escape is just as important as executing the mission.

### 1. Recognizing Alert Stages

- **Suspicion (Yellow Alert)** – Guards investigate strange noises or movement.

- **Detected (Orange Alert)** – If spotted, guards will actively search the area.

- **High Alert (Red Alert)** – If an alarm is triggered, guards will call reinforcements or lock down exits.

## 2. Best Escape Tactics

- **Use Hidden Routes** – Find vents, underground tunnels, or rooftops for alternative exits.

- **Change Your Path** – Avoid running straight to the escape zone if enemies are chasing you.

- **Break Line of Sight** – Hide behind objects, enter locked rooms, or use smoke bombs to disappear.

- **Split Up If Needed** – If playing with a team, splitting up can confuse enemies and increase survival chances.

Avoiding detection is always better than dealing with its consequences.

# 7.4 Using the Environment to Your Advantage

Every heist environment in *Monaco 2* offers opportunities for smart players to manipulate and control the situation.

# 1. Environmental Tools & Features

- **Ventilation Shafts** – Great for sneaking past guards and avoiding main hallways.

- **Hackable Doors & Alarms** – The Hacker can turn security systems against enemies.

- **Light & Shadow Mechanics** – Stick to dark areas to reduce visibility.

- **Breakable Objects** – Some walls, windows, and barriers can be destroyed for new escape routes.

# 2. Using NPCs & AI Behavior

- **Blending In** – Some characters can disguise themselves, moving through restricted areas.

- **Triggering NPC Reactions** – Some civilians will panic and alert guards, while others might serve as distractions.

Mastering the environment gives players a tactical advantage in every heist.

# Chapter 8: Multiplayer & Co-op Play

## 8.1 How to Play Multiplayer

Multiplayer in *Monaco 2* brings a new level of strategy, teamwork, and excitement to heists. Playing cooperatively with friends or other players allows for more creative approaches to missions but also requires coordination to avoid chaos.

### 1. Multiplayer Game Modes

- **Co-op Mode** – Players work together to complete heists, sharing loot and responsibilities.

- **Versus Mode (if available)** – Compete against other teams in completing objectives faster or sabotaging the enemy crew.

- **Challenge Mode** – Special multiplayer challenges with unique modifiers and harder difficulty.

### 2. How to Join a Multiplayer Session

- **Quick Match** – Find and join a public lobby with other players.

- **Private Lobby** – Invite friends to a session for coordinated gameplay.

- **LAN/Local Co-op** – Play with others on the same network or split-screen (if supported).

# 8.2 Setting Up Private Sessions & Lobbies

Creating a private lobby lets you play with friends without random players joining.

## 1. How to Create a Private Lobby

- Select **Multiplayer Mode** from the main menu.

- Choose **Create Private Lobby** and set your session settings.

- Invite players from your friend list or share a session code.

- Adjust difficulty settings, mission selection, and custom rules.

## 2. Customizing Multiplayer Settings

- **Difficulty Adjustments** – Modify enemy AI, security response, or time limits.

- **Friendly Fire** – Enable or disable damage from teammates.

- **Loot Sharing** – Choose between shared or individual loot rewards.

- **Respawn Rules** – Adjust how players can revive or rejoin a mission if eliminated.

# 8.3 Communication & Team Roles

Good communication is key to executing successful multiplayer heists.

## 1. Best Communication Methods

- **Voice Chat (Recommended)** – Talk in real time to coordinate actions.

- **Ping System** – Mark points of interest like doors, guards, or loot spots.

- **Pre-Planning** – Discuss the strategy before starting a mission to assign roles and responsibilities.

## 2. Defining Team Roles

A well-organized team should distribute tasks efficiently:

- **The Hacker** – Disables cameras, security systems, and electronic doors.

- **The Cleaner** – Takes out guards silently and controls high-alert situations.

- **The Pickpocket** – Moves quickly through levels, collecting loot efficiently.

- **The Mole** – Creates new paths by breaking walls and bypassing security barriers.

- **The Gentleman** – Uses disguises and deception to move unnoticed.

# 8.4 Tips for Success in Co-op Heists

## 1. Stick to the Plan

- Before starting a mission, assign tasks to each player.

- Avoid chaotic actions like rushing ahead without backup.

- Identify escape routes in case the mission goes wrong.

## 2. Avoiding Accidental Detection

- One careless mistake can compromise the entire heist.

- Move carefully and be aware of teammates' locations.

- Use distractions strategically instead of panicking when spotted.

## 3. Synchronizing Actions

- Have players complete multiple tasks at once (e.g., one hacking while another steals loot).

- Communicate before opening doors or disabling security systems.

- Cover each other's escape when alarms trigger.

## 4. Adapting When Plans Go Wrong

- If the mission gets compromised, stay calm and adapt.

- Use smoke bombs, disguises, or alternate exits.

- Prioritize mission completion over unnecessary fights.

# Chapter 9: Secrets, Easter Eggs, and Unlockables

## 9.1 Hidden Areas & Secret Missions

*Monaco 2* is filled with hidden locations and secret challenges that reward players for exploration and curiosity.

### 1. How to Find Hidden Areas

- **Use the Mole's Ability** – Some walls can be broken to reveal secret rooms.

- **Look for Unmarked Doors** – Some levels contain locked doors that don't appear on the main map.

- **Listen for Audio Clues** – Strange noises or NPC dialogue can hint at hidden areas.

- **Interact with the Environment** – Certain objects can be moved to reveal passageways.

### 2. Secret Missions & How to Unlock Them

- **Complete Main Story Missions** – Some secret levels unlock after finishing key story objectives.

- **Achieve High Scores** – Completing heists with top rankings can reveal bonus missions.

- **Find Hidden Collectibles** – Some missions contain rare items that open up new heists.

## 9.2 Easter Eggs & Fun References

*Monaco 2* is known for its clever nods to pop culture, gaming history, and even real-world heists.

### 1. Notable Easter Eggs

- **Classic Monaco Callbacks** – Hidden locations reference the original *Monaco: What's Yours Is Mine.*

- **Pop Culture References** – Look out for nods to famous movies, books, and real-life heist stories.

- **Developer Secrets** – Some areas contain inside jokes or special messages from the developers.

### 2. How to Find Easter Eggs

- **Explore Non-Essential Areas** – Some references are placed in rooms not required for mission completion.

- **Interact with NPCs** – Certain characters may say lines referencing other games or media.

- **Experiment with Unusual Actions** – Using tools in unexpected ways can sometimes trigger hidden surprises.

## 9.3 Achievements & Trophies

Earning achievements in *Monaco 2* adds an extra challenge for completionists.

# 1. Categories of Achievements

- **Story-Based** – Completing major heists unlocks standard achievements.

- **Skill-Based** – Stealth-only runs, speed runs, and perfect heists (no alarms triggered).

- **Exploration** – Discovering hidden areas, secret NPCs, or collecting special items.

- **Multiplayer Challenges** – Completing missions cooperatively or under specific conditions.

# 2. Notable Achievements & How to Earn Them

- **Ghost Master** – Complete a heist without being detected once.

- **Speed Demon** – Finish a mission under a strict time limit.

- **Treasure Hunter** – Find all hidden collectibles in the game.

- **Teamwork Triumph** – Successfully complete a multiplayer heist with all players escaping together.

# 9.4 Unlocking Bonus Content

Beyond story missions, *Monaco 2* features bonus content that adds depth and variety to gameplay.

## 1. Unlockable Characters & Skins

- **Challenge Missions** – Completing difficult heists unlocks exclusive character skins.

- **Secret Heist Objectives** – Some characters are only available after meeting hidden requirements.

- **In-Game Currency** – Certain cosmetics and bonus content may be purchasable with heist earnings.

## 2. Custom Game Modes & Extra Features

- **Hardcore Mode** – A challenging mode with permadeath and stricter enemy AI.

- **Community Challenges** – Special developer-made or community-submitted heists.

- **Speedrun Mode** – Timed challenges for leaderboard rankings.

# Chapter 10: Troubleshooting & FAQs

## 10.1 Common Bugs & Fixes

Even the best games have occasional technical issues. Here are some of the most common problems players encounter in *Monaco 2* and how to resolve them.

### 1. Game Crashes & Freezes

- **Issue:** The game crashes on startup or during gameplay.

- **Fix:**

    - Ensure your graphics drivers are up to date.

    - Run the game as an administrator.

    - Verify game files through Steam/Epic launcher.

    - Lower graphics settings if experiencing performance issues.

### 2. Connection & Multiplayer Issues

- **Issue:** Can't connect to online matches or private lobbies.

- **Fix:**

- Check your internet connection and router settings.

- Ensure firewall/antivirus isn't blocking the game.

- Restart the game and reattempt lobby creation.

- Use a wired connection instead of Wi-Fi for stability.

## 3. Audio/Visual Glitches

- **Issue:** Sound missing or graphical glitches appear.

- **Fix:**

  - Adjust audio settings in-game and ensure drivers are updated.

  - Toggle V-Sync or change resolution settings.

  - Run the game in windowed mode if fullscreen causes issues.

## 4. Save Data Issues

- **Issue:** Progress not saving properly.

- **Fix:**

  - Ensure cloud save is enabled if using a cloud service.

  - Check game file integrity in the launcher.

○ Manually back up save files if needed.

# 10.2 Performance & Optimization Tips

For a smoother gameplay experience, consider these optimization techniques.

## 1. Best Settings for Performance

- **Resolution Scaling** – Lowering this can boost FPS significantly.

- **Shadows & Lighting Effects** – Reducing these settings improves performance.

- **V-Sync & Frame Rate Limits** – Enable or disable depending on your hardware.

## 2. Improving Load Times

- **Install on an SSD** – Faster read speeds help reduce loading times.

- **Close Background Applications** – Free up system resources by shutting down unnecessary apps.

- **Reduce Graphics Quality** – Especially helpful for older systems.

### 3. Increasing Multiplayer Stability

- **Use a Wired Connection** – More stable than Wi-Fi.

- **Select Closest Server Region** – Lower ping and better connection quality.

- **Disable Background Downloads** – Prevent bandwidth-heavy applications from interfering.

## 10.3 Frequently Asked Questions

Here are answers to some of the most common questions about *Monaco 2*.

### 1. Is *Monaco 2* Cross-Platform?

- **Answer:** Check official updates, but currently, cross-platform play may be limited to specific platforms.

### 2. How Many Players Can Play in Multiplayer?

- **Answer:** The game supports up to 4 players in co-op, similar to the original *Monaco: What's Yours Is Mine*.

### 3. Can I Play Solo?

- **Answer:** Yes! The game is fully playable solo, though some heists are easier with a team.

### 4. Are There Mods or Custom Levels?

- **Answer:** Depending on the developers, Steam Workshop support or community mods may be available post-launch.

### 5. Does *Monaco 2* Have Controller Support?

- **Answer:** Yes, full controller support is expected. Players can switch between keyboard/mouse and controller seamlessly.

# 10.4 How to Contact Support

If you run into unresolved issues, here's how to contact the game's support team.

### 1. Official Support Channels

- **Developer Website:** Visit the official *Monaco 2* site for FAQs and troubleshooting.

- **Support Email:** Contact the support team via their listed email.

- **Game Forums & Community Pages:** Many issues are discussed and resolved on official forums.

### 2. Submitting a Bug Report

- **Provide Detailed Info** – Include platform, system specs, and a clear description of the issue.

- **Attach Screenshots/Videos** – Helps developers understand the bug better.

- **Check Patch Notes First** – Some issues might already have fixes available.

## 3. Community Support & Player Help

- **Reddit & Discord Channels** – Other players may have solutions to common problems.

- **Steam Community Discussions** – If playing on Steam, the community section often has troubleshooting threads.

www.ingramcontent.com/pod-product-compliance
Lightning Source LLC
LaVergne TN
LVHW051717050326
832903LV00032B/4251